Norma Jean

Marilyn Monroe

1945

Norma Jean

Marilyn Monroe

1945

Photography by
William Carroll

Published by Coda Publications

P.O. Box 71, Raton, New Mexico 87740 U.S.A.

ISBN 0-910390-70-3
Library of Congress Control Number

2004092064

Norma Jean

Marilyn Monroe

1945

A Day At The Beach

With Norma Jean

William Carroll

In 1945 many Southern California photographers were using my AnscoColor film processing and printing service located in Los Angeles. It was a highly personalized service and they often discussed their most recent work with me as a sharing of mutual interests. My company was expanding rapidly and had recently opened branches in Hawaii, Portland (Oregon) and in San Francisco. Our representatives needed point-of-sales material and an active project was the production of a counter-display card demonstrating the quality of our work. Our advertising agency designed a beautiful card and we decided to apply a genuine photographic color print to the card instead of relying on printing-press simulations of the photographer's art.

Concurrently with this in-house project, we had completed negotiations with the Universal Camera Company, located in New York City, to provide their dealers with color film processing services. This arrangement was to support their new camera, the Universal Mercury II, scheduled for introduction in late 1945.

Accordingly the counter-card and camera projects were merged and it was decided to do a daylong shoot with a pre-production Mercury II camera. The resulting color print, on the counter-card, would demonstrate the quality of our color printing and photographic ability of Universal's new camera. Our photo-finishing dealers and their retail camera dealers could then display the same advertising and in the doing serve two purposes: Sell film processing and Universal cameras.

As luck would have it, a pair of friendly clients, photographers David Conover and Potter Hewith (Hewitt) were using my laboratory services to process much of their work. Potter was comfortable with my mother who managed the professional services desk and he proudly showed her slides of a recent informal shoot that David Conover had completed with a personal friend named Norma Jean Dougherty. My mother, knowing of our company plans for a counter-card, called me from the office so Potter could show me the Norma Jean pictures. There was no question about how well she photographed and we primarily discussed the girl's ability to handle herself and the possible fee for modeling. These Conover pictures displayed a girl of outstanding charm. Not totally beautiful but fresh in a most delightful girl-next-door manner. And that was the exact type I wanted to decorate the point-of-purchase counter display for my laboratory services.

Potter gave me a telephone number and later that day I called her. Norma Jean asked about my method of obtaining her number and my relationship with Conover and Hewith. After she accepted my assurances of legitimacy we agreed on a fee for a day's shoot. An appointment was made for her to be picked up in West Los Angeles, at that time known as Sawtelle.

As Southern California residents may know, August was once the time for beaches and lovely women. This was, of course, in 1945 before smog destroyed Los Angeles and those of us who lived there bragged of looking miles over the sea to be sure Catalina Island was still around. Accordingly, about 8:30 on an August morning, bright and sunny as expected, I headed off toward the Pacific coastal area. On the way I was to meet this unknown, and untried, model known as Norma Jean Dougherty.

As I neared her home address, the thought uppermost in my mind was, "Will she come off as well for me as she did for Conover?"

The address, on Nebraska Avenue, was one block south of Santa Monica Boulevard, at the corner of Cotner Avenue. I lucked out and found the numbers on garage-over apartments at the first try. As I drove into the parking area, looking upward to find the right apartment, a curtain was pulled aside for a moment before the door opened and a pleasantly well-built girl waved at me. She backed out of the apartment, locked the door and hurried along the balcony toward the stairs.

"She appears straight, from here," I thought. "Nice of her to be on time."

I opened the passenger door of my wheels and watched silently while she tossed clothes onto the back seat and planted her makeup case on the front seat between us. She hopped in, closed the door solidly and smiled a "Good morning." I thanked her for being ready. As we drove toward the beach, on Santa Monica Boulevard, she commented on my car, a Mercury "Woody" station wagon, and compared it to something she was driving. Our conversation was non-committal and it seemed obvious she was waiting to decide where I was coming from. At Santa Monica's Palisades we turned down the ramp to Pacific Coast Highway near the Jonathon Club and headed north along the beach toward Malibu.

By now, following my usual procedure with new models, I had told Norma Jean about the shoot, why it was being done, what we wanted to accomplish and asked for her opinions on how best to do it. Her major suggestions were to keep the shots informal and stay away from bathing suits so we would not offend mom and pop users of photographic services.

I noticed her wedding ring and we talked a bit about our private lives. It appeared that she was handling problems but there was no poor mouthing or solicitations for sympathy. I had recently gone through an emotional divorce and shared a few of my thoughts. Neither of us were heavy on details. From today's viewpoint (1988 when these notes were drafted) Norma Jean and I were more philosophizing than complaining.

Our shoot location, one I had enjoyed for years, was the now non-existent Castle Rock. As a lad I had bicycled there on weekends and sat high on the rock, about 20-feet above the adjacent highway, to toss overripe tomatoes at passing cars. This was great fun until one day a targeted car stopped and the driver, fully ten-feet tall, threatened to paddle my buns into pulp if I ever threw another tomato. Years later, as a photographer, it had been a most useful location site for beach pictures. It was far enough from Santa Monica and Sunset boulevards to be a relatively private beachfront area that was seldom used by bathers.

I pulled up near the Rock and backed onto a parking area so Norma Jean could use the rear of the wagon for dressing. After inspecting the beach site, she pointed out that she could more easily change clothes on the beach within a tiny opening in the bluff's facing. Then we worked our way down the steep pathway, she with clothes and case in hand and I with camera and minor pieces of equipment.

On the beach she perched on a boulder half buried in the wet sand and opened her case to complete makeup and sharpen her lips. I asked if we could shoot informals and she grinned and told me to go ahead. Thusly began a comfortable relationship that continued throughout the entire day's work. I began shooting while she combed, then added pictures while she tied a scarf over her head because of the strong sea breeze, and we were off. Clothes were switched frequently as she posed on the sand, on a tiny mound near the boulder and against Castle Rock. The longer we worked, the easier it became. Norma Jean was a refreshing natural. When she moved into position, it was so rapidly as though she was reading my mind. Then, after hearing the camera click, she would modify the pose to give me something fresh and brightly new.

It should be emphasized; these resulting pictures are Norma Jean's. The best I did was to keep the camera active and shift us around for the best light.

About noon we agreed to being hungry. Everything was hauled up the narrow path, dropped into the back of the station wagon and we drove off toward Santa Monica. About a block north of where Sunset Boulevard ended at Pacific Coast Highway we parked in a genuine drive-in restaurant with attractive young women who brought orders to your car on trays that were hung from the car-door sill after the window was down.

There was nothing original about our lunch: Hamburgers, malts and fries. Again we discussed personal problems, more freely than when we had first met. Finally talked out and well fed. full, we returned to Castle Rock with adequate time for additional shooting. On the beach, with more changes of clothing and fresh ideas for posing, everything was going well until the camera jammed around the film. It was an untested prototype and I should have carried a spare camera, but none were available from the early stages of production.

The question then became: How could we safely remove exposed film from the camera on that sunlit beach…without ruining the existing pictures?

Luckily Norma Jean had worn a pair of hounds-tooth wool slacks that had been replaced with white shorts when we began work. I had been wearing a jacket that was discarded at the same time. Putting the two together solved the problem. I borrowed her slacks, pulled up the zipper, laid slacks on the sand and put the camera inside. Norma Jean rolled the waistband down a few inches and held it tightly closed. I covered her hands and the upper section of the slacks, with my jacket. Then I pulled each leg of the slacks up and over my arms, somewhat like putting on a coat the wrong way. My hands and camera, inside her slacks, were somewhat protected from the sun by the fabrics of our discarded clothing.

While she held everything together against the sea breeze, I opened the camera body inside this improvised dark room and rolled the 35mm film back into its metal cassette. That I was not fully successful was demonstrated by a few images that displayed a yellow colorcast from being slightly exposed to sunlight seeping through my jacket and her slacks.

Mission accomplished, we returned to work with much shared laughter about my being inside her slacks on a public beach. Nicest of all, there was nothing really personal about our jests. Our comfort level was such that erotic suggestions were ignored in favor of enjoying humor of the situation.

More film was exposed for excellent photographs, in afternoon light, to gain some of the best pictures taken that day. Finally we were both exhausted. I drove Norma Jean to her home and paid for her modeling services.

"How much?"
Twenty dollars for the day.

Often asked is "What was she like?"
In this area there are two answers.

During my years as a professional photographer I have exposed film on at least 200 female subjects. But Norma Jean is one of the very few for whom today's memories are clear and defined. She was impressive, to say the least. My day at the beach was a rewarding visit with a delightful young woman who was articulate, intelligent and eager to do the very best she could. Her conversation was relative and opinions expressed were those of a person who had something genuine to offer.

The second answer is for those of a more mundane nature; Norma Jean was a good model and a friendly person with which to share a hamburger.

I never saw her, nor heard from her, after this day.

"So what kind of a woman was Marilyn Monroe?"
I don't know.

W.C.

Addendum:

The preceding material was first prepared in 1988, based on notes from my business files. The shooting film, from which both color and monotone prints are based, was 35mm Kodachrome Daylight processed by Eastman Kodak in their Hollywood laboratory in 1945. I had selected Kodachrome because the dye-former grain structure was much finer that the best of AnscoColor. No filtration was used during the shoot and all images display a light bluish haze in shadow detail. Film images are one-half the standard 35mm image size, or about one-inch high by ¾-inch wide. One image was selected and my laboratory made 300 prints on Ansco Printon. They were excellent and the single remaining copy is, in 2004, nearly as well balanced as current color prints on modern photographic materials.

It is also worth noting that from 1945 until late in 1987 the slide-mounted images were buried amid photographic files containing thousands of other pictures. It was only after reading about the 1987 auction of informal Marilyn Monroe photographs taken by David Conover, in which pictures she is wearing the same clothes used during our Castle Rock shoot, that I became aware of the Monroe association. This resulted in a four-month search through my film files to find these images, now herein for the first time published.

From "A Day At The Beach, With Norma Jean."

W.C.

Marilyn Monroe 1945   *William Carroll*

Marilyn Monroe 1945   William Carroll

Marilyn Monroe 1945　　　　　　　　　　　　　　　　　　　　　　　　*William Carroll*

Marilyn Monroe 1945   *William Carroll*

Marilyn Monroe 1945

William Carroll

A custom color print of the image on the reverse of
this page, as thumbnailed on the back cover,
is available under image Number MM4-42

Image Copyright property of William Carroll

Marilyn Monroe 1945   *William Carroll*

A custom color print of the image on the reverse of
this page, as thumbnailed on the back cover,
is available under image Number MM71

Coda Publications, POBox 71, Raton, New Mexico 87740 USA

Marilyn Monroe 1945 *William Carroll*

Marilyn Monroe 1945   *William Carroll*

Marilyn Monroe 1945   *William Carroll*

Marilyn Monroe 1945   *William Carroll*

Marilyn Monroe 1945   *William Carroll*

Marilyn Monroe 1945   *William Carroll*

Marilyn Monroe 1945   *William Carroll*

Marilyn Monroe 1945

A custom color print of the image on the reverse of
this page, as thumbnailed on the back cover,
is available under image Number MM83

Image Copyright property of William Carroll

Coda Publications, POBox 71, Raton, New Mexico 87740 USA

Marilyn Monroe 1945   *William Carroll*

Marilyn Monroe 1945   *William Carroll*

A custom color print of the image on the reverse of
this page, as thumbnailed on the back cover,
is available under image Number MM24

Image Copyright property of William Carroll

Coda Publications, POBox 71, Raton, New Mexico 87740 USA

Marilyn Monroe 1945   William Carroll

A custom color print of the image on the reverse of
this page, as thumbnailed on the back cover,
is available under image Number MM47

Marilyn Monroe 1945   *William Carroll*

Marilyn Monroe 1945   *William Carroll*

A custom color print of the image on the reverse of
this page, as thumbnailed on the back cover,
is available under image Number MM29

Coda Publications, POBox 71, Raton, New Mexico 87740 USA

August 5, 1962

Marilyn Monroe 1945   *William Carroll*

Printed in the United States
65350LVS00006B/169-216

9 780910 390712